PIANO | VOCAL | GUITAR

LORDE

MELODRAMA

ISBN 978-1-5400-0260-0

HAL•LEONARD®

7777 W. BLUEMOUND RD. P.O. BOX 13819 MILWAUKEE, WI 53213

In Australia Contact:
Hal Leonard Australia Pty. Ltd.
4 Lentara Court
Cheltenham, Victoria, 3192 Australia
Email: ausadmin@halleonard.com.au

Visit Hal Leonard Online at
www.halleonard.com

CONTENTS

GREEN LIGHT

Words and Music by ELLA YELICH-O'CONNOR,
JACK ANTONOFF and JOEL LITTLE

Moderate Pop beat

I do my make-up in _____ some-bod-y else-'s car. _____

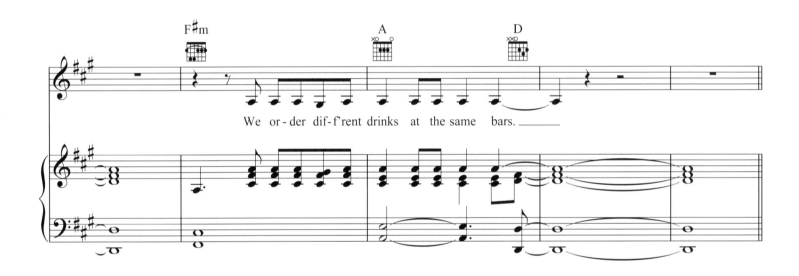

We or-der dif-f'rent drinks at the same bars. _____

I know a-bout what you did, and I wan-na scream the truth. _____
Some-times I wake up in _____ a dif-f'rent bed - room. _____

SOBER

Words and Music by ELLA YELICH-O'CONNOR
and JACK ANTONOFF

Moody Pop

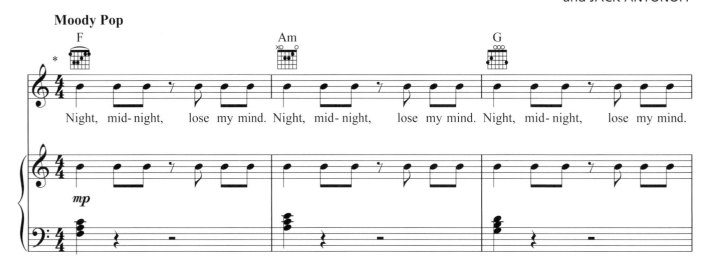

Night, mid-night, lose my mind. Night, mid-night, lose my mind. Night, mid-night, lose my mind.

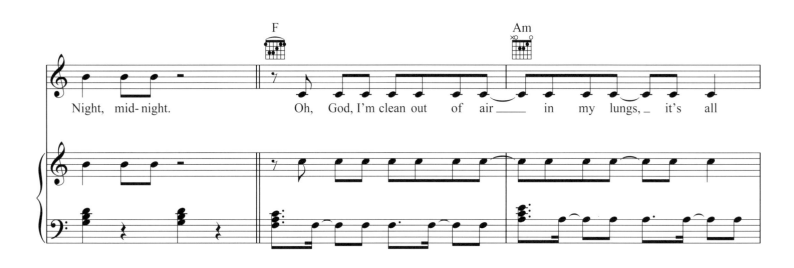

Night, mid-night. Oh, God, I'm clean out of air in my lungs, it's all

gone. Played it so non-cha-lant, it's time we danced with the truth.

* Recorded a half-step lower

HOMEMADE DYNAMITE

Words and Music by ELLA YELICH-O'CONNOR,
JAKOB JERLSTRÖM, LUDVIG SÖDERBERG
and TOVE LO

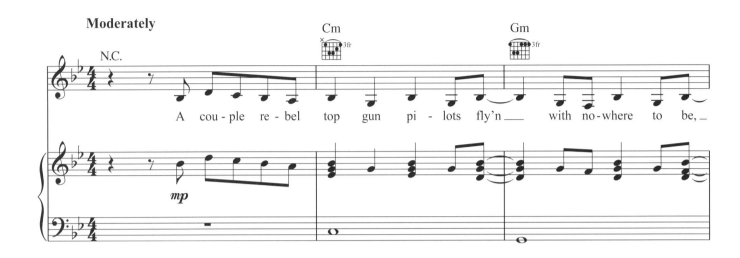

A cou-ple re-bel top gun pi-lots fly'n ___ with no-where to be, ___

___ ooh. ___ Don't know you sup-er well but I think that you

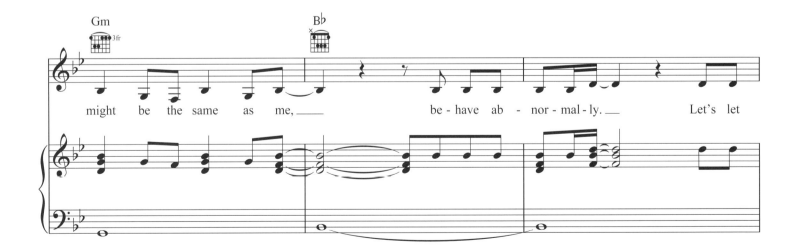

might be the same as me, ___ be-have ab-nor-mal-ly. ___ Let's let

THE LOUVRE

Words and Music by ELLA YELICH-O'CONNOR
and JACK ANTONOFF

*Lead vocal written an octave higher.

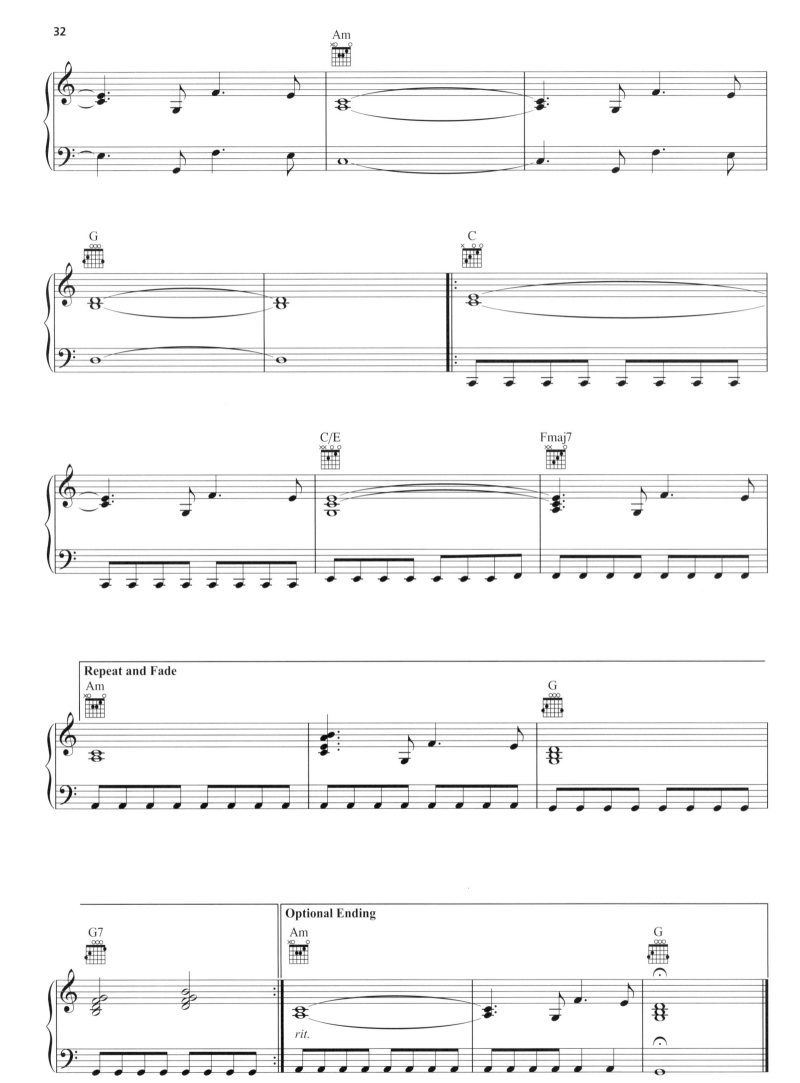

LIABILITY

Words and Music by ELLA YELICH-O'CONNOR
and JACK ANTONOFF

* Recorded a half step lower.
** Vocal written one octave higher than sung.

HARD FEELINGS/LOVELESS

Words and Music by ELLA YELICH-O'CONNOR
and JACK ANTONOFF

Moderate groove

*"Hard Feelings" recorded a half step higher.

Moderate Dance beat
"LOVELESS"

Bet you wan-na rip my heart out. ___ Bet you wan-na skip my

calls now. ___ Well, guess what? ___ I like that. ___ 'Cause I'm gon-na mess your

SOBER II
(Melodrama)

Words and Music by ELLA YELICH-O'CONNOR
and JACK ANTONOFF

You asked if I was feel-ing it? — I'm psy-cho high. Know you won't re-mem-ber in the morn-ing when I speak — my mind. — Lights are on — and they've — gone home, — but

* Recorded a half step lower.

WRITER IN THE DARK

Words and Music by ELLA YELICH-O'CONNOR
and JACK ANTONOFF

Break the news you're walk-ing out _____ to be a good man for some-one else. _____

Sor-ry I was nev-er good ___ like you.

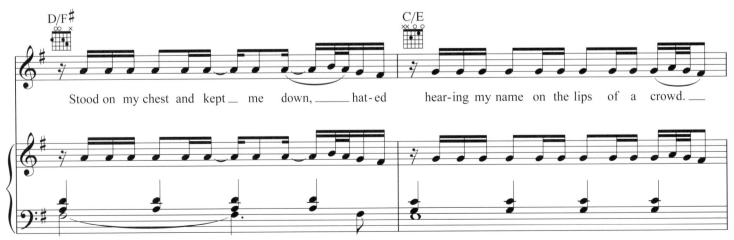

Stood on my chest and kept ___ me down, _____ hat-ed hear-ing my name on the lips of a crowd. ___

Lead vocal written an octave higher.

SUPERCUT

Words and Music by ELLA YELICH-O'CONNOR
and JACK ANTONOFF

In my head, I play a su-per-cut__ of

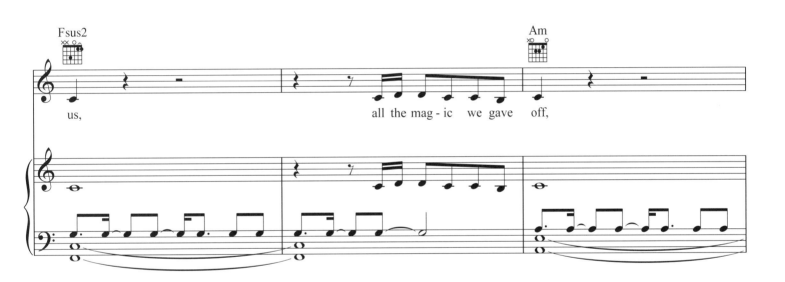

us, all the mag-ic we gave off,

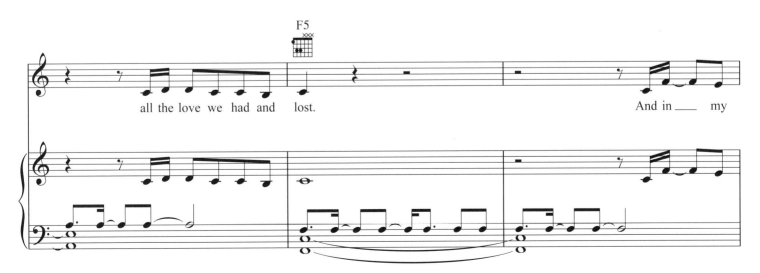

all the love we had and lost. And in__ my

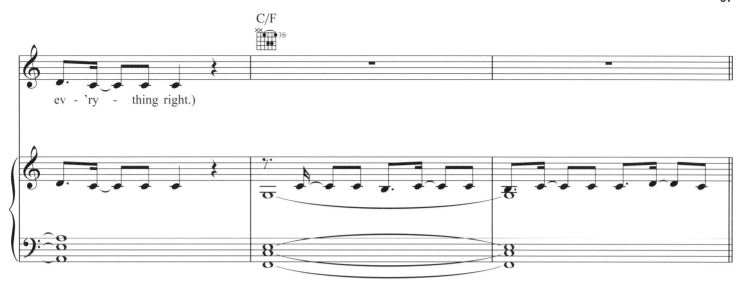

ev - 'ry - thing right.)

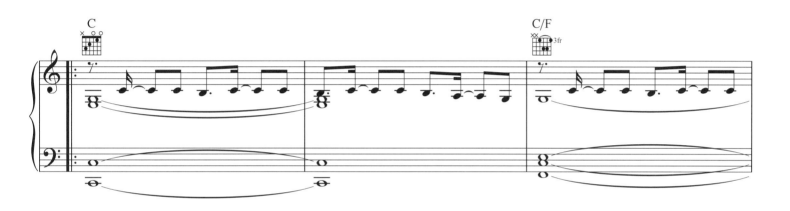

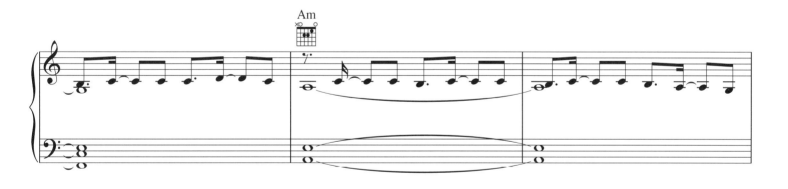

Repeat ad lib.

Final Ending

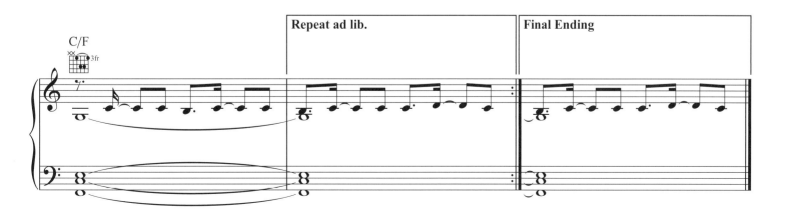

LIABILITY
(Reprise)

Words and Music by ELLA YELICH-O'CONNOR
and JACK ANTONOFF

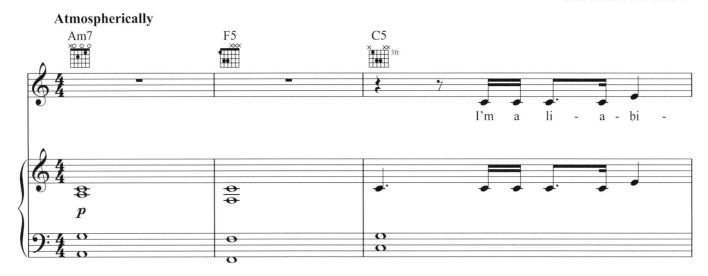

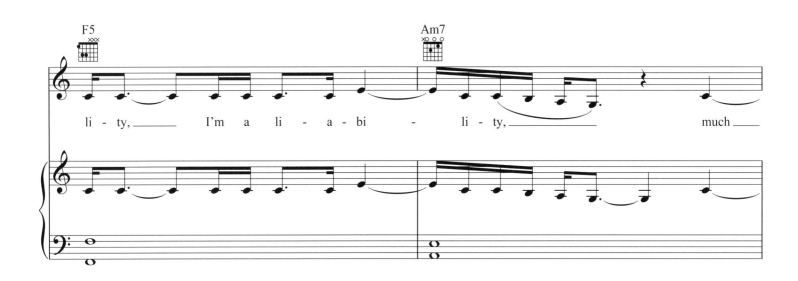

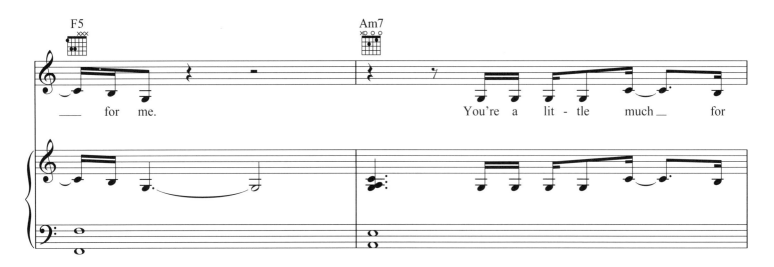

PERFECT PLACES

Words and Music by ELLA YELICH-O'CONNOR
and JACK ANTONOFF

Moderate Pop

Ev-'ry night _ I live and die, _ feel the par - ty to my bones. Watch the wast - ers blow the speak - ers, spill my guts be - neath the out - door light. _ It's